21ST
Century
Skills Library

ANIMAL INVADERS
ZEBRA MUSSEL

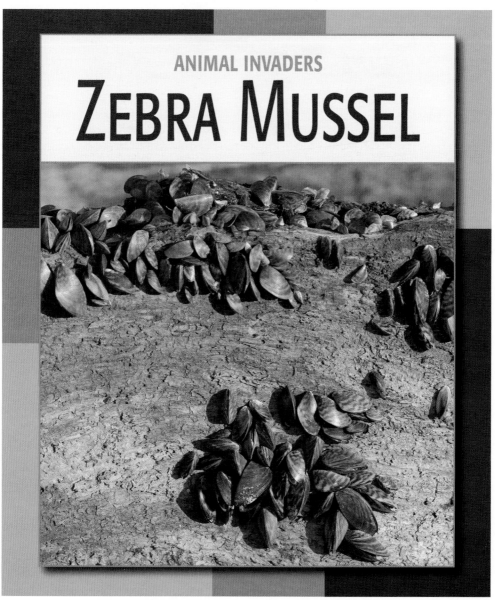

Susan H. Gray

Cherry Lake Publishing
Ann Arbor, Michigan

Published in the United States of America by Cherry Lake Publishing
Ann Arbor, MI
www.cherrylakepublishing.com

Content Adviser: Professor Thomas G. Horvath, Director, Environmental Sciences
Program, Biology Department, SUNY-Oneonta, Oneonta, New York

Please note: Our map is as up-to-date as possible at the time of publication.

Photo Credits: Cover and page 1, © Whitney Cranshaw, Colorado State University,
Bugwood.org; pages 4, 7, and 11, © U.S. Geological Survey Archive, U.S. Geological
Survey, Bugwood.org; pages 5 and 8, © Maximilian Weinzierl/Alamy; page 12, © Randy
Westbrooks, U.S. Geological Survey, Bugwood.org; pages 13 and 24, © aaron peterson.
net/Alamy; page 14, © Andreas G. Karelias, used under license from Shutterstock, Inc.;
page 17, © iStockphoto.com/BehindTheLens; pages 19 and 22, © David P. Lewis, used
under license from Shutterstock, Inc.; page 20, © blickwinkel/Alamy

Map by XNR Productions Inc.

Library of Congress Cataloging-in-Publication Data
Gray, Susan Heinrichs.
Zebra mussel / by Susan H. Gray.
   p. cm.—(Animal invaders)
ISBN-13: 978-1-60279-111-4
ISBN-10: 1-60279-111-2
1. Zebra mussel—Juvenile literature. I. Title. II. Series.
QL430.7.D8G73 2008
594'.4—dc22   2007033512

Cherry Lake Publishing would like to acknowledge the work of
The Partnership for 21st Century Skills.
Please visit www.21stcenturyskills.org for more information.

TABLE OF CONTENTS

CHAPTER ONE

SETTLING DOWN

Zebra mussels are triangular in shape.

A tiny zebra mussel (*Dreissena polymorpha*) creeps along the lake floor. Its shell is opened just enough for its little foot to poke through. The foot reaches out and presses down on the sand. The shell drags up behind. Reach, press, drag. Reach, press, drag.

These zebra mussels have attached to a stone underwater.

Progress is slow. Finally, the mussel stops. It has found the perfect spot—a nice, hard rock. The mussel attaches tightly to the rock. If all goes well, the mussel will stay here for the rest of its life.

Zebra mussels are considered an invasive species. But what exactly is that? Something invasive has invaded a place. It has moved in and taken over. Human activity usually brings in an invasive species.

A species is a particular kind of plant or animal. Tulips, blue jays, and zebra mussels are different species. Invasive species, then, are living things that have come into new areas and have flourished. If they have no natural enemies in their new homes, they spread quickly. Quite often, they are called pests. Zebra mussels have invaded bodies of water in North America. Can you think of any invasive species in your area?

What is a mussel? A mussel is a soft-bodied animal that lives in a shell. The shell has two parts that are held together at a hinge. Packed inside the shell is the mussel's body.

The zebra mussel body includes organs that sense light and movement, organs that process food, and organs that circulate water. Strong muscles allow the shell to open and close. So you might say that mussels have muscles!

CHAPTER TWO

TINY MUSSELS GROW UP

Zebra mussels can measure about 1 inch (2.5 centimeters) long.

Zebra mussels are small, shelled animals that grow no larger than a human thumb. At one time, they were found only in the seas of southwest Russia. Now they are found in other parts of Asia, as well as in Europe and North America. They live in freshwater lakes, streams, and rivers.

*Can you see the dark byssal threads that the zebra
mussels use to fasten themselves to larger things?*

Each mussel starts life as a tiny, free-floating animal.
When temperatures rise in the spring and summer, adult
female mussels release thousands of egg cells into the
water. The adult males release sperm cells at about the
same time.

When an egg cell and a sperm cell join, they form a new, very tiny zebra mussel. These undeveloped forms are called larvae.

A zebra mussel larva looks nothing like its parents. It is so small, it can be seen only with a microscope. It is clear, with no shell. Its short, hairlike structures flutter constantly, sweeping bits of food into its tiny body.

When the mussel grows a little bigger, it develops a small, round shell. But that does not make it heavy enough to sink. The mussel is still no bigger than the head of a pin. So it continues to float along in the water.

In time, the mussel develops a single, fleshy foot. About this time, it sinks to the floor of the lake or river. Using its foot, it creeps along until it finds something hard or sturdy enough on which to attach.

The zebra mussel then puts out dozens of tough threads from an organ in its foot. These are called byssal threads.

They cling tightly to the hard object, firmly anchoring the mussel in place. If the animal is knocked free, it grows new threads and latches on to a new spot. But once a mussel attaches, it usually stays put.

As the settled mussel grows, its shell develops into a triangular shape. Some shells are black or tan in color. But most are tan with black stripes. The stripes are either straight or zigzagged. It is this striped shell for which the zebra mussel is named.

Once settled, the mussel feeds by drawing water into a tube and filtering the food out. Food might include tiny plants and animals that float in the water. It might also include bacteria or even some smaller zebra mussels. Water, sand, and other nonfoods flow out of another tube.

Little mussels often settle on the shells of other, bigger zebra mussels. In fact, mussels can become stacked, layer upon layer, with the oldest ones on bottom and the youngest on top. Over time, those at the lowest

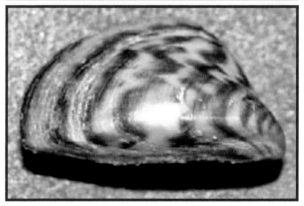

The zebra mussel shell comes in several different colors and patterns. The shell is most often striped like a zebra.

*Tiny zebra mussels grow on a bigger mussel
in layers, crowding each other out.*

layers begin to die. Water circulation is poor at the bottom
of the heap, and they cannot get enough food.

Zebra mussels have few natural enemies in North
America. Fish larvae eat zebra mussel larvae. Older mussels
become food for some ducks and adult fish. However,
predators never really eat that many mussels. So in North
America, zebra mussel numbers just keep rising.

CHAPTER THREE

INVADING MUSSELS

*Empty zebra mussel shells cover the Lake Michigan
shoreline near Gulliver, Michigan. These broken shells
can easily cut into the bare feet of beachgoers.*

Zebra mussels don't have to do much to invade new lakes.
They simply live and multiply. They either drift or are
drawn into new places.

When the water temperature is at least 54 degrees
Fahrenheit (12 degrees Celsius), males and females release

their sperm and egg cells. One female can release tens of thousands of egg cells at a time. A small colony of mussels can produce billions of tiny larvae.

These young larvae are not strong swimmers. They are swept along with waves and currents. Quite often, they are sucked into water pipes on ships. This is probably how zebra mussels came to North America.

Large cargo ships fill their hulls with water before long trips. This load of water, called **ballast**, keeps a ship from being top-heavy. Ballast keeps the ships balanced for trips across the ocean. When these ships reach their destination, they unload their cargo and dump the water in their hulls. This water can be loaded with millions of young zebra mussels.

In 1988, mussels were discovered in Lake Saint Clair, which lies between Canada and the United States. It is likely that a ship in Europe took on ballast water and

Large cargo ships often carry seawater in their hulls to balance the vessel. At the end of their trip, they dump the water. Ships from Europe probably brought zebra mussels to North America in this way.

crossed the Atlantic Ocean. When it reached North America, it sailed down the Saint Lawrence River. When the ship finally stopped, it dumped the ballast water loaded

with zebra mussels. The mussels now had a new home. They had space in which to grow and spread. They had plenty of food. And they had left most of their predators behind.

What's more, people did not know much about these mussels and did things to help the mussels spread. For example, when people went fishing, they filled their bait buckets with lake water containing young zebra mussels. As the people moved about on the lake, they might have dumped that water, helping the mussels to spread even farther.

Boaters soon spread the mussels to other lakes. Young zebra mussels use their byssal threads to cling to boats and

*Fishers and boaters can transfer zebra mussels to
other lakes without being aware of it.*

motors. When owners haul their boats from the water,
thousands of mussels can be attached. In damp weather,
the mussels live for several days out of water. So when
boaters visit another lake, the mussels fall from the boat
and soon spread throughout the new body of water.

Centuries ago, the mussels were only in two seas bordering Russia—the Caspian and Black seas. But zebra mussels have been riding along in ballast water, in bait buckets, and on the sides of boats for a few hundred years. This is probably how they spread from Russia to Europe to North America.

In the United States, zebra mussels made their way into all of the Great Lakes and into the Mississippi River. From these waters, they continued to spread outward. Most recently, zebra mussels were reported as far west as Nevada!

CHAPTER FOUR

WHAT'S THE PROBLEM?

A woman at Ontario's Charleston Lake Provincial Park holds a stick covered with zebra mussels.

Once the mussels move in, they have plenty to eat and other animals feed on them. So what is the problem? Why would anyone try to get rid of them?

In their new homes, zebra mussels have few natural enemies. Ducks and only a few fish feed on them. But a small group of mussels can produce millions of young every year. There are soon far more mussels than the predators can eat.

When zebra mussels bind to aquatic animals, they can keep the animals from moving and eating.

Both young and old mussels eat by filtering the water for food. They actually make the water clearer.

While clear water may sound like a good thing, it can cause other problems. Lakes and rivers are teeming with tiny floating plants and animals called **plankton**. Plankton can be so thick they cloud the water. But fish, clams, and other animals feed on plankton. Once the zebra mussels move in, they spread quickly and hog the food. Fish that eat plankton starve to death, and animals that eat *those* fish soon die.

Zebra mussels can cause the death of **aquatic** animals in other ways. They can attach to clams, crayfish, or water turtles. They suck food away from the clams. They cover crayfish and keep them from moving normally. Zebra mussels can weigh a turtle down so that it cannot come up for air.

Zebra mussels also attach to buoys, the large floats that mark dangerous spots in the water or safe sailing routes. But the sheer weight of the mussels can sink these important warning devices.

Scientists often keep track of the clarity, or clearness, of lake water. Many have noticed that the clarity improves when zebra mussels move in and eat all the tiny plants and animals that normally float around. When the water becomes clearer, sunlight reaches deeper into the lake. How might this affect plants growing on the lake bottom?

Zebra mussels damage many of the structures they attach to, including wooden boat docks and concrete bridges.

Even the tiny, floating larvae are troublesome. They are easily drawn into water pipes. The larvae settle, attach, and grow there. In time, they grow large enough to clog the pipes. The pipes might lead to a building full of firefighting equipment. Fire hoses will fill up with the mussels. When it comes time to put out a fire, the hoses will have only a weak spray.

Or the larvae might travel up water pipes that lead into boat engines. The engines can quickly overheat because the pipes carrying their cooling water are jammed with mussels.

But the biggest problem occurs when the water pipes lead to large plants that purify water for people's homes. These pipes are great places for mussels to settle and grow. Water is constantly flowing into the pipes, so the animals have an unlimited food supply flowing right to them. Workers have discovered mussels tightly crammed into the pipes. At one plant, more than a half million mussels were packed into an area the size of a bath towel!

Learning & Innovation Skills

Scientists have found that zebra mussels prefer to attach to water pipes that are horizontal—those that are lying down. They attach less often to pipes that are vertical—those that are standing up. Why do you think the mussels prefer horizontal pipes?

CHAPTER FIVE

CONTROLLING THE SPREAD

People have used electric currents to help control the spread of zebra mussels. These researchers are using a similar method to monitor fish in Michigan.

Today, many efforts are underway to control the spread of zebra mussels. One approach is for people to wash their boats down with hot water or leave them out in the sun to dry before visiting other lakes. They can also scrape mussels and plants from the hull. In fact, it is against the law in some states to leave lake weeds on the hull of a boat.

People are also working to keep the mussels out of water-purifying stations, factories, and power plants. They have installed filters and screens in water pipes. Blasting the systems with high-pressure water hoses has helped. People have also tried running very hot water and electrical currents through the system to keep out or kill off the mussels.

At some water-purifying stations, the pipes have copper coatings. Zebra mussels will not cling to pipes lined with copper. Other places are using pipes coated with very slippery paint so the mussels cannot latch on.

Some people have thought of using chemicals to poison or ward off the mussels. However, chemicals must be used with great care. It is difficult to find a chemical that harms only the mussels without hurting other species.

In trying to deal with invasive species, scientists often look to other countries where those species live. So how have Europeans dealt with the zebra mussel? After all, zebra mussels spread into Europe much earlier than they did into North America.

Unfortunately, Europeans have not solved the problem, either. Predators in some European lakes are doing a pretty good job, however. Certain ducks are now helping to keep the mussels under control. Some have changed their **migration** paths in response to the mussels. Now, during their yearly migrations, the ducks stop at lakes where they can eat their fill of mussels. The mussel numbers drop while the ducks are there. But in the following months, the numbers go back up again. It seems that the ducks are just barely able to keep the mussels under control.

In North America, a few duck species feed on the mussels. However, these ducks have small populations. There just aren't enough of them to keep the mussel numbers down.

Right now, many scientists are working on ways to control zebra mussels. They have a big job because the mussels continue to spread. Perhaps one day, human beings will discover the secret to controlling these little invaders.

Zebra mussels do perform one important job. They provide researchers with information about the level of poisons and chemicals in a lake. Each mussel filters about 1 quart (about 1 liter) of water every day. Its body takes in whatever chemicals might be in the water. By examining the mussels closely, scientists interested in water quality can learn valuable information about how clean or polluted the lake water is. To make progress in their fields, researchers must use all available resources.

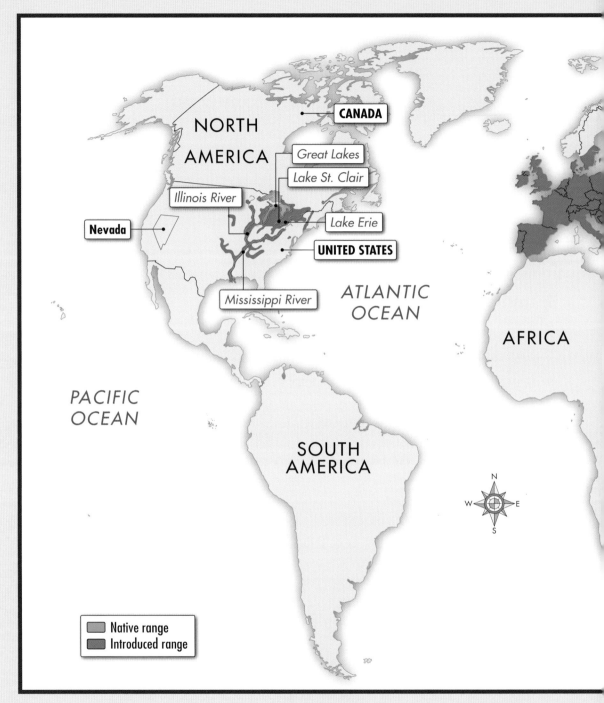

NORTH
AMERICA

CANADA

Great Lakes

Lake St. Clair

Illinois River

Nevada

Lake Erie

UNITED STATES

Mississippi River

ATLANTIC
OCEAN

AFRICA

PACIFIC
OCEAN

SOUTH
AMERICA

N
W   E
S

Native range
Introduced range

This map shows where in the world the zebra mussel

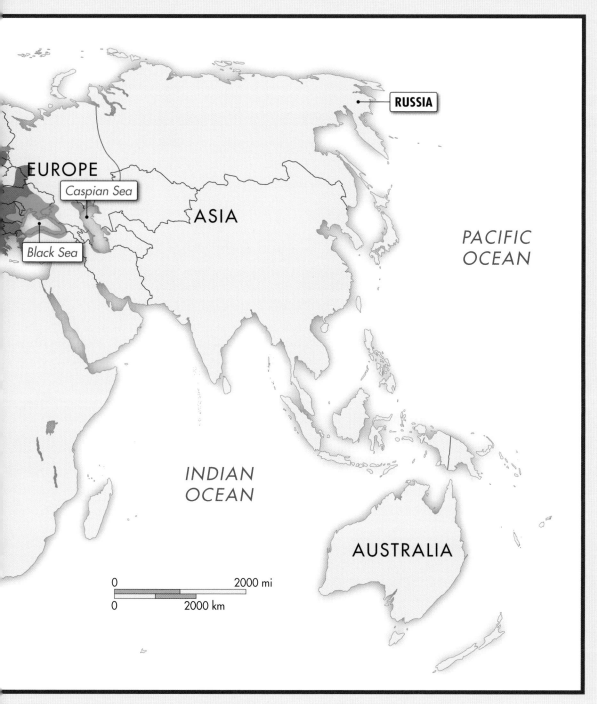

RUSSIA

EUROPE

Caspian Sea

ASIA

Black Sea

PACIFIC
OCEAN

INDIAN
OCEAN

AUSTRALIA

0   2000 mi

0   2000 km

lives naturally and where it has invaded.

Glossary

aquatic (uh-KWAH-tik) living in water

bacteria (bak-TIR-ee-uh) microscopic living things that are made up of only a single cell

ballast (BAL-uhst) a heavy substance, such as water or sand, that a ship carries to improve its stability

byssal threads (BISS-uhl THREDZ) one of many tough threads on a mussel's foot that help the animal cling to a surface

egg cells (EG SELZ) special cells released by female animals that combine with sperm cells from males to form a new animal

larvae (LAR-vee) very young, undeveloped forms of certain animals such as mussels

migration (my-GRAY-shuhn) a major trip that is made at the same time every year

plankton (PLANK-tun) tiny floating plants and animals

predators (PRED-uh-turz) animals that hunt and eat other animals

species (SPEE-sheez) a group of similar plants or animals

sperm cells (SPURM SELZ) special cells released by male animals that combine with egg cells from females to form a new animal

FOR MORE INFORMATION

Books

May, Suellen. *Invasive Aquatic and Wetland Animals*. New York: Chelsea House, 2007.

St. Antoine, Sara. *The Great Lakes: A Literary Field Guide*.
Minneapolis: Milkweed Editions, 2005.

Stewart, Melissa. *Life in a Lake*. Minneapolis: Lerner Publications, 2003.

Web Sites

Dynamic Map of Zebra Mussel Distribution
www.atlas.usgs.gov/dynamic/an_zm.html
For an excellent map that shows how zebra mussels have
spread through the United States over time

Sea Grant: National Aquatic Nuisance Species Clearinghouse
www.aquaticinvaders.org/nan_ld.cfm
For an international library of research, government policies, and education
publications about invasive sea and freshwater aquatic animals in North America

USGS: Frequently Asked Questions About the Zebra Mussel
cars.er.usgs.gov/Nonindigenous_Species/Zebra_mussel_FAQs/zebra_mussel_faqs.html
To learn more from the U.S. Geological Survey about zebra mussels

INDEX

ABOUT THE AUTHOR

Susan H. Gray has a master's degree in zoology. She has written more than 70 science and reference books for children, and especially loves writing about animals. Gray also likes to garden and play the piano. She lives in Cabot, Arkansas, with her husband, Michael, and many pets.